The Gift To Be Simple Bread Book

...a Door County journey with recipes

Carol and Bill Hoehn

Illustrated by Roberta Larson

Dancing Bears' Press
Fish Creek, Wisconsin

First Edition

ISBN: 0-942495-48-9

Library of Congress Catalog Card Number: 95-69439

Published by
Dancing Bears' Press
N8732 Highway F
Fish Creek, Wisconsin 54212

Printed by
Palmer Publications, Inc.
PO Box 296
Amherst, Wisconsin 54406

Back cover photography by Harmann Studio

Journeys begin with dreams.......

Tis The Gift To Be Simple, Tis the Gift To Be Free.

Tis the Gift to Come Down Where you Ought to Be

And When You Find Yourself in the Place Just Right

Twill Be in the Valley of Love and Delight

When True Simplicity is Gained,

To Bow and to Bend We Shan't Be Ashamed

To Turn, Turn, Will Be Our Delight,

Til By Turning, Turning We Come Round Right.

— Shaker Hymn

Like many of the visitors to The Gift To Be Simple Gallery, our journey to Door County took many twists and turns before we settled in the "place just right." We had to unlearn many city ways to fit into the lifestyle of those who already knew the quality of Door County ways. This book is dedicated to the many friends and family with whom we have shared a loaf of bread and jug of wine, who make life rich and overflowing. It is a book about honest bread with genuine flavors and great character. As you bake these breads we want you to dream of this thumb of rock and water and for a few moments, wander away from keys and car alarms. Join us in our land of delight.

Carol and I began our journey to Door County on our honeymoon in 1969. We lived the rest of the year dreaming of life in the wild, in the midst of an artist colony away from shopping malls, traffic, city schedules and dead bolts. We looked at a romantic farmstead in the country and suggested to our family that this place would be ideal for all future family vacations. "No? How can you say no?" Next year the property increased in value making it even less accessible. Ten years later, we found a small home in Ellison Bay. The real estate agents were overwhelmingly happy to sell a "handyman special" listed on the last page of the MLS book. Carol's dad kicked the foundation like a used car and declared he would not give $50 for the whole thing. Half a bottle of Jack Daniels and four hours later, her parents agreed to loan us the down payment for the former lodge of the Mystic Workers of the World, a life assurance society for orchardmen. We left our jobs in Ft. Wayne and moved in after 19 days of renovation. We always did like camping. I began to finish my dissertation. We both took jobs that left us time to enjoy piney smells, velvet air and shaking winds. We both learned to spin, Carol took time to paint. We met every sort of artist and character who used to have a very important job. All of us lived on Door County time which is at least two weeks slower than expectations.

After finishing my Ph.D., I was able to get a one-year teaching post in Two Rivers, so we commuted on the weekends back to Ellison Bay. Carol loved the sound of the fog horn in "Trivers" and spent her time teaching dance, painting her quilt square designs, and making our Bear of the Month ornaments. Our journeys back and forth taught us that in small towns, inquiring minds really do want to know who got a ticket for going 80 mph in a 55 mph zone..."and they are teachers too, an so"... and that there are no public bathrooms open on Sunday nights from Baileys Harbor to the Mill Supper Club in Sturgeon Bay no matter how hot the salsa is.

The next leg of our journey was to the Twin Cities to take up teaching positions in St. Paul and Minneapolis. Our time in the cities was filled with all the best the best of cities can offer. And yet, we felt incomplete and out of touch with the sounds of waves and sea gulls, the howls of coyotes and snorts of deer. As our friends waxed rhapsodic about the sunset over an inland lake ringed with orderly asphalt lanes, we could only picture the technicolor majesty of a sunset view from the Clearing Bluff in Ellison Bay. During a cookout behind our apartment, we looked up and noticed that half the world was gone; no sky, no stars, no satellites streaking, no moon, nothing but grayish haze from the street lights. How different from cosmic power of dancing northern lights with all their aerie coils snaking and pulsing right there for all to see in the brightly polished Door County sky.

As the old proverb says, "Be careful what you wish for, you may get it." I was caught in a reduction of staff at my school. Two days later, a friend called from Door County. Four days later I had a teaching position in Sturgeon Bay. Three months later we journeyed home to Ellison Bay.

By November 1984, we purchased a 135-year-old farm between Baileys Harbor and Fish Creek. It was set in the midst of a pine tree farm surrounded by open meadows with deer, raccoons, porcupines, fox, skunks, rabbits, very vocal coyotes, sandhill cranes, Canada geese, ruffed grouse and one very cocky pheasant. The farm house was built by a Welsh Irish sympathizer who talked a bit too much, feared for his life, and fled to Wisconsin. We hear tales about nine children being raised in the house at one time even though it now fits just the two of us. Actually there are four of us, counting our children Mr. Tygge (18 lbs. tabby, handsome but not too bright) and Willow (6 lbs...., silvery grey, fancies herself a Russian Blue, demands that her name be prefaced with "the Beautiful Miss...", very bright, very deadly.) The property is still referred to as "the old Williams place" despite there having been at least three owners since the Williams. How long it will take to become "the old Hoehn place?"

We went just a lot silly with 20 acres on which to play and set about planting gardens nourished with enough manure for five farms. Carol's nightmares about manure pirates getting her coveted pile of prime, aged horse road apples from down the road played right into my plan of getting a real country beat up truck. All the fertilizer produced bumper crops from the 56 tomato plants, six zucchini hills, potatoes, and every vegetable and herb we knew to grow. We now practice ZZPG...zero zucchini population growth by planting only one hill.

We learned that a ten cord load of wood logs will remain an accusing testament to naivete for a very long time. Pine snakes always get their way. Skunks live in apple boxes in the shed but so do baby kittens. Apples with extra protein don't make the fresh cider any less sweet. And unlocked doors encourage the mysterious appearance of fish, cheese, bread, or heaven forbid, another zucchini in the refrigerator. Our life in Door County continues to be a journey.

We travel many hours between home and Sturgeon Bay or Green Bay to our teaching jobs. But coming home always includes the ritual of getting out of the car, sniffing the cool air carrying strong sweet scents of wood smoke, apples, and wildflowers, looking at the Milky Way stretched like a beckoning grin across the sky, and saying to each other, "Lord, this is heaven, isn't it." A quick hug, a 30-second version of bears dancing in the moonlight, and it's back inside to cuddle by the fire before we begin anew our journey in Door County.

INTRODUCTION

In 1981, we opened our shop, The Gift To Be Simple Gallery, in a rehabbed chicken coop next to the Griffin Inn. Carol sold her needlework kits, dough ornaments and other treasures. To attract customers, we sat in front spinning at the wheel and kept a fish boil pot full of reeds simmering over an open fire. "Local color"...that's what some folks said about us. For a neophyte in a land where local means your daddy's mama's mama was born here, achieving "local color" status was a stunning accomplishment.

The Gift To Be Simple found its home in the Settlement Shops for two years. Carol's painting on quilt squares evolved into intricate painting on finished clothing. Drawing on her extensive work with theatre costumes, she created painted and hand-sewn garments that have earned acclaim. Her works can be found in museum and bank shows and many private holdings. The summers became an endless series of trips between home and shop for water, lunch, paints, thread and other supplies. We dreamed of having a shop at home with a large work space inside and an English cottage garden outside. With the help of my school colleague, we built the present classic barn and the business came home. Now welcoming visitors to the shop is like inviting them into our home.

At The Gift To Be Simple, we want to give to our visitors the same kind of joy of discovery we felt when we were visitors to Door County. On our vacations, potters, glassblowers, weavers and watercolorists all shared glimpses of their arts and made us feel the art we purchased was only for us. Every Thursday in July and August our friends and fellow artists demonstrate their arts under the umbrella of Wolf River apple trees and offer visitors a chance to wander the paths in the pines or read a book, paint a picture or just sit quietly in the woods. To make the moment more sensual, we offer freshly baked bread, herbed butter, and minted lemonade. The bread is baked in an outdoor wood fired oven a friend of mine and I built from a description of a native American adobe oven.

A description of a simple bread oven is given in Bernard Clayton, *Complete Book of Breads* (Simon and Schuster). Clayton's oven is made of adobe; a material not suited to Wisconsin. George Hardiman, a potter friend, and I used fire brick and concrete instead of plain brick and adobe. Between layers of cement on the arch of the oven, a blanket of insulation keeps the heat in the oven. I fire the oven with good hard wood (iron wood, maple, or oak) and let the fire burn hard for 2-3 hours so the concrete mass is heat saturated. After shoveling all the wood and ashes out of the oven, I set a rectangular baking stone on bricks to keep the bread from burning on the oven floor. By opening or closing the wooden door, the temperature can be kept to a hot 400 degrees. We can maintain baking temperature for about 4-5 hours, although the last few loaves do take a long time to finish.

At The Gift To Be Simple, we bake bread for fun. We have no intention of selling it or going commercial. Bread baking should not be a complicated technical process. We start with a basic recipe and, by the addition of ordinary ingredients, produce breads with great texture and flavor. The European style crust we get by using the wood fired oven can be produced in an ordinary oven with very simple techniques. As you bake these breads, relax...have fun. Try your own variations. Remember, "tis the gift to be free."

As Bill says in the introduction, "tis a gift to be free," ...excellent advice to bread makers. Few endeavors are more creative, satisfying, and forgiving of minor variations.

In our early married life, a neighbor, who worked in landscape design, saw me worrying over the few bulbs and seeds I could squeeze into our limited yard space. He advised, "Relax, Carol. Things WANT to grow." So does bread! Practice makes confidence and everyone will enjoy eating the mistakes anyway.

On baking days, I drag out the flour and yeast, open the fridge and pantry to see what's there to recreate the taste of something we have eaten in New York, or Los Angeles, or Mexico. Bill often has something in his head that he wants to reach his taste buds. If you start with the basic proportions of flour, yeast, and liquid, you can substitute various flours, liquids and seasonings to create your own special loaves.

Use bread flour when called for. It is now widely available in most grocery stores. All purpose flour is also fine.

Heat all liquids to the temperature specified in the recipe. Overheating will cause the yeast to die. Cooler temperatures will only slow the rising process. I use a microwave for heating and check with a thermometer.

Bulk yeast is available in the health food section of many grocery stores. It is usually fresher and less expensive than packaged yeast.

In our recipes, we use large grade A eggs.

Dry milk or buttermilk powder and an equivalent amount of water may be used whenever milk or buttermilk is required.

To knead bread, turn the wet dough onto a lightly floured surface. Work the dough into a rough ball with floured hands. Fold the dough in half and push it down hard away from you. Turn the dough a quarter of a turn and repeat the folding and pushing until the dough becomes smooth and elastic. Really throw your weight into it instead of just using your arm muscles. As the dough develops, carbon dioxide produced by the yeast is trapped by the gluten strands which helps the bread rise with a wonderful texture. For therapy, work the dough by slamming it against the surface occasionally. If you get tired, let the dough rest for a few minutes and then get back at it.

Use a metal or plastic dough scraper to gather up the dough and add sprinkles of flour if the dough gets too sticky.

A common mistake for beginners is adding too much flour. Too much flour will make the finished loaf dry and heavy. When the dough is ready, it will feel smooth, hold its shape on the kneading surface, and spring back when you press two fingers into it.

Before setting aside to rise, be sure to cover the dough with plastic wrap or a damp kitchen towel. Let the dough rise in a warm place. We have a wood heated stove in our house so it is an ideal place for raising dough. A warm kitchen, a sunny place (safe from marauding animals) or near your oven are good places to use. If it is cool, the dough will just rise more slowly. If you need to stop the process of bread making, you can even put the dough in the refrigerator overnight. When you bring the dough out into a warm kitchen in the morning, it will continue to rise normally.

Punch down the dough with your fist after the first rising before shaping the loaves.

Adjust baking times and temperatures for your own oven. If the bread is browning too quickly, tent aluminum foil over the top and lower the temperature 25 degrees. Check frequently. I often use a higher than usual oven temperature when I use baking tiles or stones.

Oven or pizza stones can be purchased in many cookware shops, but unglazed quarry tiles may also be used to achieve a beautiful European-style crust. The stones can be arranged to fit your own oven and are quite inexpensive. Baking stones should be placed in the oven 45 minutes to an hour prior to baking. If the bread is placed on a well-floured peel or cookie sheet, you can slide the risen loaf onto the tiles with a quick jerk (and a little practice).

Follow the individual recipe instructions for spraying techniques. You may want to adjust the oven temperatures lower after the three mistings to avoid over-browning. The steam allows higher initial temperatures and a crisper crust.

Any recipe can be shaped as you choose, baked in bread pans, on cookie sheets or on baking tiles.

Resist, yes, I said resist the temptation to cut into the hot fragrant loaf just out of the oven. It continues to bake for several minutes longer. But we all break the rules and besides who cares if the bread is a little gummy when the fresh butter melts into it?

Menu...

....a Door County Journey with Recipes

...Sweet Breads...

...Flat breads...

...to make bread less alone...

...Too Wonderful Beverages
to go with the loaf and thou...

Recipes...

Farmhouse Basic White Bread

Yields 2 loaves

1/4	cup margarine
2	cups milk plus additional milk for topping
4-5	cups bread flour, divided
1	cup instant potato flakes
2	tablespoons dry yeast
3	tablespoons sugar
1	tablespoon salt
1/4	teaspoon ginger

Heat margarine and milk together in saucepan to 130-140 degrees. Margarine does not have to be completely melted. Mix 3 cups flour and all other dry ingredients. Add milk and margarine mixture. Beat 2 minutes in a mixer or by hand. Gradually add 1-2 cups additional flour until a soft dough forms.

Turn out onto floured surface and knead 8-10 minutes or until smooth and elastic. Sprinkle with additional flour as needed. Place in greased bowl, turning to coat. Cover with towel and let rise 45-60 minutes or until doubled in volume. Punch down dough and let rest for 5 minutes.

Shape dough into 2 loaves and place in greased 8- by 4-inch bread pans. Let rise for 30-45 minutes until dough rises at least 1 inch above bread pan. Brush tops with milk.

Bake 30-35 minutes in 350-degree oven. If necessary, tent with foil to prevent over-browning.

Peasant Bread

Yields 3 long loaves

For sponge:

1 1/2	tablespoons yeast
2	cups lukewarm water (85-105 degrees)
1/4	cup barley malt syrup (available in the health food section of the grocery) or substitute an equal amount of light or dark corn syrup
3	cups white bread flour
2	eggs

For bread:

1 1/2	tablespoons coarse salt
3-4	cups additional white bread flour

Sprinkle yeast on water in large bowl. Stir to dissolve. Add syrup and mix completely. Add 3 cups flour and eggs, and beat 4-5 minutes to develop gluten. Cover and set in a warm place for 1-2 hours. After the initial sponge rising, add salt and additional flour to make a soft dough.

Knead on floured surface until dough is smooth and elastic, adding small amounts of flour as necessary. This can take 8-10 minutes or less as the sponge makes it easier to knead. Place in greased bowl, turn to coat, and let rise 1-1 1/2 hours.

Punch down, divide into 3 pieces, and let rest 10 minutes. Shape into 3 long loaves 14- by 3-inches long. Place in greased baguette pans or on greased cookie sheet. Cover and let rise 45-60 minutes.

Preheat oven to 375 degrees and bake 25-30 minutes until golden. Cool before serving.

Lukes' Lighthouse Rye

Yields 3 loaves

Roy and Charlotte Lukes, naturalists, authors, and artists, share many of our interests. The one notable exception is our devotion to the species felidae, which is obviously in direct competition with their passion for birds. They have been stalwarts of Bill's church choir at Immanuel Lutheran, and Wednesday nights mean time for Charlotte's notorious puns. In fact no matter how tired we all may be when we get to practice, by the time we have laughed and sung for an hour we all know why we do it. Choir parties are invariably pot luck hors d'oeuvre extravaganzas with John Brann's blender brought along for Brandy Alexanders. We shamelessly admit parties have been used to lure new members to our ranks.

The Lukes have graciously allowed us to include their recipe. Roy baked it in the old range light at the Ridges. Now if they can just forgive me for noting that Willow cat's favorite ice cream flavor is "Chickadee Swirl."

1	12-ounce bottle beer
1 1/2	cups buttermilk
3	tablespoons butter or margarine
6	tablespoons sugar
1 1/2	teaspoons salt
1	tablespoon caraway seeds
2	1 1/4-ounce packages dry yeast
5	cups white flour
4	cups medium rye flour

Heat beer, buttermilk, and butter until butter melts, stirring constantly. Cool to 115 degrees. Add sugar, salt, and caraway seeds and mix well. Add yeast and stir until dissolved. Add 1 cup each of white and rye flour and mix well. Add 1 cup of each alternately until a stiff dough is formed.

Turn onto floured board. Cover and allow to rest 5 minutes. Knead for 10 minutes adding more flour as needed. Place in a greased bowl and turn to grease all sides. Cover and let rise until doubled in volume. Punch down and shape into 3 round loaves. Place in greased pie pans.

Cover and let rise until nearly doubled.

Bake in preheated oven at 400 degrees for 30 minutes. Turn down heat to 350 degrees and bake an additional 15 minutes. Bread should be crusty with a soft, fine inside.

Spinach Bread with Garlic and Rosemary

Yields 2 round loaves

5-6	cups white bread flour, divided
2	tablespoons dry yeast
1	tablespoon salt
2	tablespoons sugar
1	tablespoon peeled, chopped garlic
1	teaspoon garlic powder
1/4	cup chopped fresh rosemary or 2 tablespoons dried rosemary, slightly crushed
1	10-ounce package frozen chopped spinach, thawed
	Additional water
3	tablespoons olive oil plus additional oil for brushing
	Kosher salt

Mix 4 cups flour, yeast, salt, sugar, chopped garlic, garlic powder, and rosemary in large bowl. Add enough water to thawed spinach to make 2 cups total liquid and vegetable. Heat mixture to 120-130 degrees. The microwave works well for this. Add liquid and olive oil to dry ingredients and mix well, 2 minutes by electric mixer or 100 strong strokes by hand. Add additional flour, 1/2 cup at a time, until soft dough forms.

Turn dough onto floured surface and knead 10-12 minutes or until dough springs back when pressed with 2 fingers. Put dough into oiled bowl, turn to coat surface and cover with damp towel or plastic wrap. Let rise in warm place until doubled in volume. Punch down, knead briefly, 10-15 strokes and let rest 5 minutes.

Preheat oven to 450 degrees and place baking stones or tiles in oven 45-60 minutes before baking.

Divide dough in half and shape each half into a round loaf. Place on well floured cookie sheet or bread peel, cover with towel and let loaves rise a second time until doubled in volume, approximately 45 minutes. In summer, or in a warm kitchen, this can take much less time!

When loaves are ready, slash tops 3 times 1/2-inch deep with a razor or VERY sharp knife. Brush tops with olive oil and dust lightly with Kosher salt.

Slide loaves onto preheated stones, or place on baking sheets on middle rack of oven. Spray entire oven interior, including bread, with water for 30 seconds. Do not spray directly on oven light bulb. Close door and bake for 3 minutes. Spray again for 30 seconds and bake for 3 minutes. Lower oven temperature to 375 degrees and bake 25-30 minutes more or until bread sounds hollow when thumped on the bottom. Let loaves cool a little before slicing.

George and Gloria often have summer dinners with us. One time we will do the main course, dessert and wine and they will bring appetizer, and salad. The next time we reverse the contributions. One evening, Carol made a torta from sliced baking potatoes, red onion rings, grated Gruyere cheese, olive oil, coarse black pepper, and lots of Greek olives all scented with rosemary leaves, baked to a crusty light amber and presented a la Potatoes Anna with a sprig of fresh rosemary as garnish. When George crossed the threshold, he was momentarily speechless, an unnatural event of the first order. The intense aroma of herb and olives was truly to be worshiped. Like one caught up with zeal, George ever after proclaimed his devotion to this dish.

The Potato Bread with Black Olives and Rosemary is a worthy substitute for George's beloved torta.

You may have caught on to our devotion to olives of all sorts. Please understand, that to get these pungent little salty gems, we have to make a Brady Street run to Milwaukee. Anyone who goes to Cream City is begged to stop at Glorioso Italian Grocery store to get what for some might be a lifetime supply of Greek, Sicilian, Kalamata, Moroccan, et al olives. If the traveler is accommodating, maybe a stop down the street for Italian cookies can be added to the agenda.

Potato Bread with Black Olives and Rosemary
(George's Bread)

Yields 2 large round loaves

1	large potato, peeled and cubed
1/2	cup semolina flour
1/2	cup whole wheat flour
5-51/2	cups white bread flour, divided
2	tablespoons yeast
1	tablespoon salt
1/4	cup dried rosemary
1/4	cup dried minced onion
2	cups hot water (130-140 degrees)
1/4	cup olive oil plus additional oil for brushing
1	cup pitted Kalamata or other black olives
	Coarse salt for brushing

Cook potato until tender and mash in a bowl. Add semolina and whole wheat flours, 3 cups white bread flour, yeast, salt, rosemary, and onion. Mix well and add hot water and olive oil. Beat well, 100 strokes by hand or 2 minutes by machine. Add olives and mix well. Add additional flour by 1/2 cups until soft dough forms.

Knead on a floured surface 9-10 minutes, adding small amounts of additional flour as necessary to prevent sticking. Place in greased bowl, turn to coat, cover, and let rise in warm place 11/2-2 hours, or until doubled in volume.

Punch down, divide into 2 pieces, and let rest for 10 minutes. Preheat oven to 400 degrees and place baking stones on oven racks. Shape dough into 2 round loaves, cover, and let rise 45-60 minutes.

Brush loaves with olive oil and sprinkle with coarse salt. Bake 20-25 minutes until bread sounds hollow when thumped on the bottom.

This bread is fun to tear apart instead of slicing. Also a great bread to dip into good olive oil.

Fresh Corn Bread with Onion and Dill

Yields 2 round loaves

4 1/2-5 1/2	cups white bread flour, divided
6	tablespoons buttermilk powder
1	cup course ground cornmeal
1	cup regular yellow cornmeal
2	tablespoons dry yeast
1	tablespoon salt
1/4	cup sugar
1	teaspoon garlic powder
2	tablespoons dried dill or
	1/4 cup chopped fresh dill
1/4	cup dried minced onion
2	tablespoons dried green pepper flakes
2	teaspoons dried celery leaves
2	cups water
1/4	cup dark molasses or corn syrup
1/4	cup margarine
1	16-ounce package frozen corn thawed, drained or
	1 15-ounce can corn, drained

Mix together 2 cups white bread flour, buttermilk powder, both cornmeals, yeast, salt, sugar and seasonings. Heat water, molasses, and margarine to 140-150 degrees. Margarine does not need to be completely melted. Beat wet and dry ingredients together 2 minutes by hand or machine. Add corn and mix in gently. Add additional flour by 1/2 cups until a soft dough forms.

Turn out onto floured surface and knead well 10-12 minutes. Dough is wet and may require more flour than usual. Place in greased bowl, turn to coat, and cover. Let rise in warm place until doubled in volume.

Preheat oven to 450 degrees and place baking stones in oven. Divide dough in half and let rest 5 minutes. Shape dough into 2 round loaves and let rise 30-45 minutes on floured sheets until doubled in volume. Slash tops with sharp knife or razor. Place loaves in preheated oven directly onto baking stones. I use a wooden bread peel for this.

Spray entire oven and bread with a plant mister for 30 seconds. Do not spray oven light. Bake 3 minutes then spray again. Repeat. Reduce heat to 375 degrees after third spraying. Continue baking for 20-25 minutes or until bread sounds hollow when tapped on the bottom.

Let cool before slicing.

Pepper Parmesan Dijon Mustard Bread

Yields 2 loaves

5-5½	cups white bread flour, divided
2	tablespoons dry yeast
1	tablespoon salt
1	tablespoon sugar
1	tablespoon coarsely ground black pepper (use less if you like a milder flavor)
1	cup grated Parmesan cheese
¼	cup Dijon mustard
2	cups hot water (120-130 degrees)
	Olive oil and Kosher salt for dusting

Mix 4 cups flour, yeast, salt, sugar, pepper, Parmesan and mustard in large bowl. Add water and mix well, 2 minutes by electric mixer or 100 strong strokes by hand. Add additional flour, ½ cup at a time, until soft dough forms. Turn dough onto a floured surface and knead 10-12 minutes or until dough springs back when pressed with 2 fingers.

Preheat oven to 450 degrees and place baking stones or tiles in oven 45-60 minutes before baking.

Put dough into oiled bowl, turn to coat surface, and cover with damp towel or plastic wrap.

Let rise in warm place until doubled in volume. Punch down, knead briefly, 10-15 strokes, and let rest for 5 minutes. Divide dough in half and shape each half into a round loaf. Place on a well floured cookie sheet or bread peel, cover with a towel, and let loaves rise a second time until doubled in volume, approximately 45 minutes. In the summer, or in a warm kitchen, this can take much less time!

When loaves are ready, slash tops three times ½-inch deep with a razor or VERY sharp knife. Brush the tops with olive oil and dust lightly with Kosher salt. Slide loaves onto preheated stones, or place baking sheets on middle rack of oven. Spray entire oven interior, including the bread, with water for 30 seconds. Do not spray directly on oven light bulb. Close door and bake for 3 minutes. Spray again for 30 seconds and bake for 3 minutes. Lower oven temperature to 375 degrees and bake 20-25 minutes more or until bread sounds hollow when thumped on the bottom. Let loaves cool a little before slicing.

Italian Loaf with Pasta Tomatoes

Yields 2 torpedo-shaped or round loaves

5-6	cups white bread flour, divided
2	tablespoons dry yeast
1	tablespoon coarse salt
2	tablespoons sugar
1	tablespoon spaghetti seasoning
1	teaspoon garlic powder
1	15-ounce can Italian-style tomatoes with peppers, onions, etc.
	or 1 15-ounce can pasta-ready tomatoes
	Water
3	tablespoons olive oil plus additional oil for brushing
	Kosher salt for topping

Mix 4 cups flour, yeast, salt, sugar, seasoning, and garlic powder. In a separate bowl, combine tomatoes, tomato liquid and water to make 2 cups total liquid and vegetable. Heat to 130-140 degrees. Add with olive oil to dry ingredients. Mix 2 minutes by mixer or 100 strokes by hand. Add pasta tomatoes and blend. Add remaining flour by 1/2 cups until soft dough is formed. Knead 8-10 minutes until dough is smooth and elastic. Add flour as necessary.

Pour into greased bowl and turn to coat. Cover and let rise in warm place until doubled in volume.

Punch down and let rest for 5 minutes. Divide dough into 2 pieces and shape into torpedo or round loaves. Let rise until doubled in volume.

Slash tops with sharp knife or razor. Brush with olive oil and sprinkle with Kosher salt.

Bake in a preheated 450-degree oven. Spray entire oven and bread 30 seconds with a plant mister. Bake 3 minutes, then spray again. Repeat. Reduce heat to 375 degrees after the third spraying. Continue baking for 25-30 minutes or until bread sounds hollow when tapped on the bottom. Tent foil over the bread to prevent over-browning if necessary.

Let cool before slicing.

Mexican Enchilada Loaf with Cumin and Peppers

Yields 3 baguettes

5-6	cups bread flour, divided
2	tablespoons yeast
1	tablespoon salt
2	tablespoons sugar
1	tablespoon cumin seed, slightly crushed
3	tablespoons dried oregano
1	15-ounce can mild or hot enchilada sauce
1	2.5-ounce can diced green chilies, drained

Combine 4 cups flour and all ingredients except chilies and beat for 2 minutes. Add chilies and beat briefly, 15-30 seconds, to blend. Add additional flour by 1/2 cups until a soft dough forms. Knead by hand or mixer 8-12 minutes. Add flour as necessary.

Place in greased bowl and turn to coat. Let rise until doubled in volume. Punch down and divide dough into 3 pieces. Let rest 5 minutes. Shape into 3 2- by 16-inch loaves or 2 long loaves. Let rise again until doubled in volume.

Place baking stones in oven and preheat to 450 degrees. Spray entire oven and bread with a plant mister for 30 seconds. Do not spray oven light. Bake 3 minutes then spray again. Repeat. Reduce heat to 400 degrees after third spraying. Continue baking for 15-20 minutes or until bread sounds hollow when tapped on the bottom.

Let cool before slicing.

Whole Wheat Herb Bread

Yields 2 loaves

2-31/2	cups white bread flour, divided
2	cups whole wheat flour
2	tablespoons dry yeast
1	tablespoon salt
1/4	cup sugar
2	teaspoons each dried summer savory, oregano, thyme, and basil or 2 tablespoons each fresh
2	tablespoons dried minced onion
1	bunch fresh parsley chopped (approximately 1 cup loosely packed)
2	cups milk
2	tablespoons olive oil

Mix 2 cups white bread flour and other dry ingredients together. Scald milk in saucepan or microwave until small bubbles form around edges then cool to 110-120 degrees. Add milk and olive oil to dry ingredients. Beat 2-3 minutes by hand or mixer. Add flour by 1/2 cups until soft dough forms. Turn out onto floured surface and knead 8-10 minutes or until dough is smooth and elastic and springs back when pushed with 2 fingers.

Place in greased bowl, turn and cover. Let loaves rise 30-45 minutes until doubled in volume. Divide dough in 2 pieces and let rest 5 minutes. Shape dough into 2 torpedo loaves, approximately 10 inches long and 5 inches wide in center, tapering at ends.

Place baking stones in oven and preheat to 450 degrees. Let rise on floured surface until doubled in volume. Slash tops with a sharp knife or razor. Place loaves in preheated oven directly onto baking stones. I use a wooden bread peel for this. Spray entire oven and bread with a plant mister for 30 seconds. Do not spray oven light. Bake 3 minutes then spray again. Repeat. Reduce heat to 375 degrees after third spraying. Continue baking for 20-25 minutes or until bread sounds hollow when tapped on the bottom. Let cool before slicing.

RLL

Roasted Seed Bread

Yields 2 long loaves

1	cup roasted, unsalted sunflower seeds
1	cup sesame seeds
1/4	cup millet seeds
1/4	cup poppy seeds
1	tablespoon nigella seeds or black caraway seeds
1/4	cup dried minced onion
4-6	cups white bread flour, divided
2	tablespoons dry yeast
1/4	cup sugar
1	tablespoon salt
2	cups hot water (130-140 degrees)
2	tablespoons corn oil

Mix all seeds and onion in a 11- by 17-inch jelly roll pan. Bake in a preheated 400-degree oven 2-4 minutes, stirring occasionally until toasted. Cool.

Mix together 4 cups flour, yeast, sugar and salt. Add hot water and corn oil and mix 2 minutes by hand or mixer. Add cooled, toasted seeds and additional flour 1/2 cup at a time until a soft dough forms.

Turn out onto floured surface and knead 8-10 minutes or until dough is smooth and elastic. (Persevere, the nuts and seeds make this a little more difficult.) Place in greased bowl, turn to coat dough, cover, and let rise 1 hour or until doubled in volume. Punch down, divide into 2 pieces and let rest for 5 minutes.

Shape into 2 long loaves approximately 4 by 14 inches and place on baking sheet which has either been lightly greased or sprinkled with cornmeal. Let rise 30-45 minutes.

Bake in a preheated 375-degree oven for 25-35 minutes. Cool on wire racks.

Note: This bread, like the Mexican Enchilada Loaf (page 10), makes incredible snack chips. Form dough into three 16-inch long loaves. Bake as per instructions. Slice cooled loaves into 1/4-inch slices and dry in a single layer on baking sheets in a 250-degree oven until crisp but not browned. Turn once. This usually takes 20-25 minutes. When cool, store in airtight bags or containers. These are a terrific alternative to fried chips for dipping or spreads. The nuts are a good source of nutrition! At least that's the way we rationalize it.

Onion Dill Bread

Yields 2 round loaves

5-6	cups white bread flour, divided
2	tablespoons dry yeast
1	tablespoon sugar
1	tablespoon salt
1/4	cup dried minced onion
1/2	cup chopped fresh dill or 2 tablespoons dried dill weed
3	scallions with green tops, finely chopped
1/4	cup margarine
2	cups hot water (130-140 degrees)

Mix 4 cups flour and all dry ingredients. Melt margarine in hot water. Add hot liquid to dry ingredients and beat in mixer 2 minutes or 100 strokes by hand. Add additional flour by 1/2 cups until a soft dough forms.

Knead 8-10 minutes, adding small amounts of flour as necessary until smooth and elastic. Place into greased bowl and turn to coat. Let rise for 45 minutes or until doubled in volume. Punch down and let rise again for 30 minutes. Punch down and shape into 2 round loaves. Let rise again on a floured peel or baking sheet.

Bake in preheated 450-degree oven. Spray entire oven and bread with a plant mister for 30 seconds. Do not spray oven light. Bake 3 minutes then spray again. Repeat. Reduce heat to 350 degrees after third spraying. Continue baking for 20-25 minutes or until bread sounds hollow when tapped on the bottom. Tent foil over bread to prevent over-browning if necessary.

Let cool before slicing.

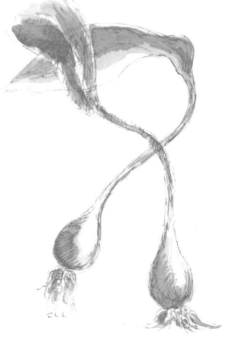

Winter Picnic

I have often wanted to produce a T-shirt with answers to the many questions visitors have about life in Door County so I could just point to a spot on the shirt and be helpful. One answer would be, "He climbs a ladder and takes them off the roof every night." The question is, "How do the goats get off the roof of Al Johnson's restaurant?" The second most asked question is "What do you do up here in the winter?" The answer to that would take a XXXL shirt. There is skiing, skating, ice fishing, ice sailing, winter walks in the parks, pot lucking, fireplace sitting, sliding down Hill 17 on inner tubes, barrel rolling down any highway (no traffic), or picnicking. If you have friends, winter, except for gray March, is a great time to be in Door County.

Winter really begins when Green Bay and the near waters of Lake Michigan freeze over. Several years ago, this coincided with our annual New Year's day rituals with Peg and John. After a night of delightful indulgences with food, wine, and friends, we got up, put on ski wear and headed for Newport State Park for the first skiing of the year. John always charges ahead leaving me with Carol and Peg. (Hey, it's a tough job but somebody's got to do it.) This particular year we also planned a full blown picnic in conjunction with the skiing. So we established a base camp for our food and gear, laid out a fire pit, put the champagne in the snow, rigged a blue tarp for wind protection and took off into the woods.

Newport Park is sometimes described as a primitive area, so warm cozy toilet houses are not to be found. Instead Carol found one of the quaint old outhouses that used to be just off the trail. Being a practical person, she decided to back into the house leaving her skis to stick under the ill-fitting door. Neither John nor I could resist rocking the house just to hear Carol laugh and scream while we watched her skis fly around as she tried to maintain her balance in a precarious position.

We like to get off the trails and play the equivalent of "chicken" by skiing down the sand dunes onto the lake ice. The winner of the game was the one who stopped with their skis the farthest over the edge of the ice mound over the water. Carol won every time although I am not sure it was a matter of technique as much as of luck. I always fell down and jammed my thumb before any critical life or water decisions needed to be made. Peg would enter into the game but John usually tried to bring a semblance of intelligence back to the group. His particular lunacy surfaced when it came to going down the forbidden hill with the big tree, large rock and impossible bend at the bottom. All of us except John were reluctant to even walk down the hill.

On the way back to the base camp we passed Europe Lake and watched the mix of ice skaters, fisherman and ice sailors revel in playing on perfectly clear smooth ice. Rinks may be fine but nothing compares to the excitement of falling down on ice and seeing straight through to the sandy bottom of a lake. One could even count the lures snagged by sticks on the bottom in the previous summer assault on the perch population.

So it was back to the camp. With paper cups of snow-chilled champagne, we built a crackling fire with only enough smoke to scent the air but not enough to prevent intimate contact with warmth. We slanted a large rock next to the fire and when it got hot, used it to melt the raclette cheese into a bubbly river of cream that coated boiled red potatoes and cornichons. The blue tarp snapped in the wind, we sat on the other side and toasted gently while Peg brought out her pot of black bean chili. More champagne, more laughter, two mugs of hot chocolate, a piece of Belgian chocolate broken off a thick bar and then it was quiet. Ice just off shore sounds like a thousand delicate wind chimes being stirred by the eternal motion of the lake. Sparks flew up from the fire and melted into a sky with more pixels of light than any television could have. An owl called from the pine tree behind us. We remained silent, closed our eyes and floated very gently in that state that is not sleep but relaxation deep enough to erase any care. That's what we did one winter.

Sundried Tomato Olive Loaves

Yields 8 soup loaves

1	cup semolina flour
3 1/2-4 1/2	cups white bread flour, divided
2	tablespoons dry yeast
1	tablespoon salt
2	tablespoons sugar
1/2	cup dried tomato bits or chopped sundried tomatoes
2	cups hot water (130-140 degrees)
3	tablespoons olive oil plus additional oil for coating
1/2	cup pitted, coarsely chopped Greek, Kalamata, or Nicoise olives
	Kosher salt for topping

Mix semolina flour, 3 cups white flour, yeast, salt, sugar, and tomato bits. Add hot water, oil and olives and mix 2 minutes by mixer or 100 strokes by hand. Add additional flour by 1/2 cups until a soft dough forms. Knead 8-10 minutes, adding small amounts of flour as necessary until a soft elastic dough forms.

Place into greased bowl and turn to coat. Let rise for 45 minutes or until doubled in volume. Punch down and let rise again for 30 minutes. Punch down and shape into 8 small, round loaves. Let rise again on floured peel or baking sheet.

Slash an 'X' into tops with a sharp knife or razor. Brush with olive oil and dust with Kosher salt.

Bake in preheated 400-degree oven. Spray entire oven and bread with a plant mister for 30 seconds. Do not spray oven light. Bake 3 minutes then spray again. Repeat. Reduce heat to 350 degrees after third spraying. Continue baking for 10-15 minutes or until bread sounds hollow when tapped on the bottom. Tent foil over bread to prevent over-browning if necessary.

Let cool before slicing.

Caraway Sauerkraut Rye Bread

Yields 2 loaves

1	cup rye flour
3 1/2-4 1/2	cups white bread flour, divided
2	tablespoons dry yeast
1	teaspoon coarse salt
1	teaspoon dill weed
1	teaspoon dill seed, slightly crushed
1	tablespoon sugar
2	teaspoons caraway seed, slightly crushed
1	8-ounce can sauerkraut with juice and enough water to make 2 cups
2	tablespoons margarine
1	egg

Mix rye flour, 3 1/2 cups bread flour and remaining dry ingredients together. Heat sauerkraut, juice, water and margarine to 130-140 degrees.

Combine sauerkraut mixture, eggs and dry ingredients and mix well, 2 minutes by electric mixer or 100 strong strokes by hand. Add additional flour 1/2 cup at a time until soft dough forms. Turn dough onto floured surface and knead 8-10 minutes or until dough springs back when pressed with 2 fingers.

Put dough into oiled bowl, turn to coat surface, and cover with damp towel or plastic wrap. Let rise in warm place 45-60 minutes until doubled in volume. Punch down and divide dough into 2 pieces to form 2 round loaves OR divide into 1 piece with 2/3 of dough and 1 piece with 1/3 of dough. Form the larger piece into a round loaf and the smaller piece into a 15-inch baguette. Let both rise 45 minutes.

Preheat oven to 450 degrees and place baking stones or tiles in oven 45-60 minutes before baking. Spray entire oven and bread with a plant mister for 30 seconds. Do not spray oven light. Bake 3 minutes then spray again. Repeat. Reduce heat to 350 degrees after third spraying. Continue baking for 15-20 minutes or until bread sounds hollow when tapped on the bottom. Tent foil over bread to prevent over-browning if necessary.

Let cool before slicing.

Note: Like any baguette-style bread, we suggest slicing the loaf into 1/4-inch rounds and gently drying them in a 250-degree oven until they are dry and crunchy. These rye chips are a perfect dipper with any cheese-based hors d'oeuvre.

Dried Vegetable Bread

Yields 2 loaves

5-6	cups white bread flour, divided
1	tablespoon Kosher salt
2	tablespoons dry yeast
1	tablespoon sugar
6-7	tablespoons buttermilk powder
1/4	cup dried onion flakes
4	tablespoons dried vegetable flakes
2	cups hot water (130-140 degrees) or substitute 2 cups buttermilk, heated, for powder and water
2	tablespoons corn oil plus additional oil for brushing

Mix 4 cups white bread flour, Kosher salt, yeast, sugar, buttermilk powder, onion and vegetable flakes. Add water and corn oil and beat 2 minutes by hand or machine. Add additional flour by 1/2 cups until soft dough forms. Turn out onto floured surface and knead 7-9 minutes or until smooth and elastic.

Place in greased bowl and turn once to coat. Cover with towel or plastic wrap. Let rise in warm place 30-45 minutes or until doubled in volume. Punch down and let rise again for 30 minutes, if you have time. If you don't, one rising is fine. Punch down again and divide into 2 portions.

Let dough rest for 5-10 minutes. Shape into 2 oblong loaves to fit 2 8- by 4-inch greased pans. Let rise a final time for 30-45 minutes. Brush tops with oil if desired.

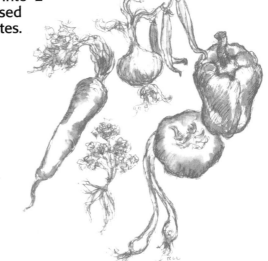

Bake in preheated 375-degree oven for 25-30 minutes or until bread sounds hollow when tapped on the bottom.

Cool before slicing.

Sicilian Sage and Olive Bread

Yields 8 round soup loaves

1	cup semolina flour
3-4	cups white bread flour, divided
2	tablespoons dry yeast
2	tablespoons sugar
2	teaspoons coarse salt
1/4	cup chopped fresh sage or 1 tablespoon dried
2	cups buttermilk
3	tablespoons olive oil plus additional oil for brushing
1	cup cracked marinated large green olives
	(1 10-ounce jar, drained and pitted)
24	fresh sage leaves for topping
	Kosher salt for dusting

Mix semolina flour, 3 cups white flour, yeast, sugar, salt, and sage. Heat buttermilk to 130-140 degrees. Add buttermilk and olive oil to dry ingredients. Beat 2 minutes. Add olives and blend completely. Add flour by 1/2 cups until a soft dough forms. Knead 9-11 minutes.

Put in greased bowl and turn to coat. Cover and let rise 45 minutes. Divide dough into 8 pieces. Form pieces into small round loaves. Press 3 fresh sage leaves into top of dough. Let rise 30-45 minutes.

Slash loaves 3 times outward from center between sage leaves. Brush top of loaves with additional olive oil and sprinkle with Kosher salt.

Bake in preheated 375-degree oven for 15-20 minutes or until loaves sound hollow when thumped on the bottom.

These loaves are wonderful with soups. Like focaccia, Sage and Olive Bread is fabulous when dipped into the highest quality olive oil.

Cinnamon Oatmeal Raisin Bread

Yields 2 loaves

2	cups oatmeal, regular or quick cooking
5-51/2	cups white bread flour, divided
2	tablespoons yeast
1	teaspoon salt
2	teaspoons cinnamon
1/3	cup sugar
2	cups milk heated to very hot (130-140 degrees)
2	eggs
1/2	cup margarine, melted
1	cup golden raisins

For glaze:
2	tablespoons sugar
1	tablespoon hot water

Mix together oatmeal, 2 cups flour, yeast, salt, cinnamon and sugar. Add milk, eggs, and margarine. Mix all ingredients for 2 minutes by machine or by hand until well blended. Add additional flour by 1/2 cups until a soft dough forms.

Turn dough onto a floured surface and knead for 10-12 minutes, kneading in raisins. This is a stiffer, heavier dough so if you get tired, just leave the dough for a few minutes and then resume the kneading. The dough doesn't care.

Place dough in greased bowl, turning to coat. Cover and let rise 1-11/2 hours in a warm place. Punch down, divide dough, and shape into 2 loaves. Place in 2 greased 9- by 5- by 3-inch pans. Let rise until doubled.

Bake at 350 degrees for 30-35 minutes. While loaves are baking, mix sugar and hot water for the glaze. Spread glaze on top of warm, baked loaves before removing from pans.

Let cool before slicing.

Pesto Swirl Bread
with Basil or Cilantro Pesto

Yields 2 loaves

1/4	cup margarine
2	cups milk plus additional milk for topping
4-5	cups bread flour, divided
1	cup instant potato flakes
2	tablespoons dry yeast
3	tablespoons sugar
1	tablespoon salt
1/4	teaspoon ginger
1	cup Basil or Cilantro Pesto (recipes follow)
1	tablespoon dried basil or cilantro for topping

Heat margarine and milk together in saucepan to 130-140 degrees. Margarine does not need to be completely melted. Mix 3 cups flour and all other dry ingredients. Add milk and margarine mixture. Beat 2 minutes in a mixer or by hand. Gradually add 1-2 cups additional flour until a soft dough forms.

Turn out onto floured surface and knead 8-10 minutes or until smooth and elastic. Sprinkle with additional flour as needed. Place in greased bowl, turning to coat. Cover with towel and let rise 45-60 minutes or until doubled in volume. Punch down dough and let rest for 5 minutes.

Divide dough into 2 pieces. Roll each piece of dough on a lightly floured surface to a 14- by 12-inch rectangle. Spread half of pesto mixture over dough leaving 1 inch uncovered on a 14-inch side. Roll tightly like a jelly roll and seal edges well. Fold each end 1 1/2 inches under and seal. Repeat with the other piece of dough and remaining filling. Place loaves in greased 9- by 5- by 3-inch pans.

Cover and let rise 30-45 minutes in a warm place. Brush with milk and dust each loaf with half the dried basil or cilantro.

Bake 30-35 minutes in 350-degree oven. If necessary, tent with foil to prevent over-browning.

Basil Pesto

Yields 1 cup

4	cloves garlic, crushed
2	cups fresh basil leaves, washed, rinsed, and dried
1/3	cup olive oil
1/2	teaspoon salt
1/2	teaspoon ground black pepper
1/4	cup grated Parmesan cheese

Put garlic and basil in food processor. With the motor running, slowly drizzle olive oil into bowl until basil is pureed. Stop motor and add salt, pepper, and cheese. Process until blended.

Cilantro Pesto

Yields 1 cup

3	cloves garlic, crushed
2	cups fresh cilantro leaves, washed, rinsed, and dried
1	tablespoon fresh lime or lemon juice
1/4	cup olive oil
1/2	teaspoon salt
1/2	teaspoon ground black pepper
1/2	cup grated Parmesan or shredded Monterey Jack cheese

Put garlic, cilantro, and lime juice in food processor. With the motor running, slowly drizzle olive oil into bowl until cilantro is pureed. Stop motor and add salt, pepper, and cheese. Process until blended.

…Filled Loaves…

Cats 1…

We admit it...we're cat co-dependent. We love them; they own us; it's hopeless. Bill was raised with dogs as pets and insisted he was allergic to my childhood cat Klyng. I suspect his attitude was prompted by Klyng's determined chaperonage while we were dating. As soon as we pulled in the driveway, Klyng would rush in and yowl, as only Siamese cats can, and wake my father who would then insist it was time for us to come in. Klyng would leap into my arms and smile with satisfaction as Bill left and he stayed to go to bed with me.

It took a tiny tabby-and-white kitten, a "party favor" sent home with a friend's child from a birthday party to change Bill's mind. Pas de quatre (Pada Cat) entered our life on my pleading. Unfortunately, I was contracted to dance for the summer in a different city so the cat bonded with Bill, and I was the "other woman" for 13 years. Pada trained us well as cat parents. We moved many times in the first years of our marriage, but she adapted cheerfully and became a commuter cat. When the suitcases appeared, she would pile her favorite toys on them, use a portable cat box, and leap up at the sight of her favorite road food restaurant. "One hamburger, hold the bun, hold the mustard, ketchup, pickle and onion."

At 6 1/2 pounds, she took on Chesapeake Bay retrievers, veterinarians, snakes and any visitors she didn't like and won every skirmish. Unfortunately, she also took a dislike to bread dough. Many a loaf, covered and rising on the warm hearth, underwent an unscheduled punch down as she happily kneaded it with her stiletto-tipped paws.

Pada's last move was to our farm. We planted a tree over the spot where she lies with her toys. She didn't approve. The tree died.

Italian Pizza Loaf with Herbs and Mozzarella

Yields 2 torpedo-shaped or round loaves

Prepare 1 recipe of Italian Loaf with Pasta Tomatoes (p. 9). After the first rising, punch down dough and divide into 2 pieces. Let rest 10 minutes.

Filling:
- 1 cup black olives (not Greek olives)
- 1/2 cup fresh parsley leaves or a combination of fresh basil, oregano, and thyme leaves
- 1 tablespoon olive oil
- 2 cups (8 ounces) shredded Mozzarella cheese

Combine all ingredients except cheese in food processor and chop very finely. Add cheese and blend together.

Roll each piece of dough on lightly floured surface to a 14- by 12-inch rectangle. Spread half of filling mixture over dough, leaving 1 inch uncovered on a 14-inch side. Roll tightly like a jelly roll and seal edges well. Fold each end 1 1/2 inches under and seal. Repeat with the other piece of dough and remaining filling. Place loaves in greased 9- by 5- by 4-inch pans.

Brush tops with olive oil and sprinkle lightly with coarse salt. Bake in preheated 350-degree oven for 25-35 minutes or until bread sounds hollow when tapped on the bottom.

Cool before serving.

Cinnamon Swirl Bread

Yields 2 loaves

5 1/2-6 1/2	cups white bread flour, divided
2	tablespoons dry yeast
1	teaspoon salt
1/2	cup sugar
1/2	cup margarine
2	cups milk
2	eggs

For filling:

1	cup dark brown sugar
1	tablespoon cinnamon
1/4	cup butter or margarine, melted

For glaze:

1	cup powdered sugar
3	tablespoons lemon juice

On Thursday demonstration days at The Gift to Be Simple, the women demand Bobbie's Chocolate Buns. But the men clamor loudly for Cinnamon Swirl Bread. They will wait and wait and wait, risking their pocket books while their wives shop, just for a hot slice of this reminiscence of maternal affection. Our friend, Richard, even plans his marathon bike treks around the time he thinks the loaf will first come from the wood oven and gets downright surly if we have not included Cinnamon Swirl on the menu for the day.

Mix 4 cups flour and remaining dry ingredients. Heat milk and margarine to 140-160 degrees. Margarine does not need to be completely melted. Add milk mixture to dry ingredients and beat 100 strokes by hand or 2 minutes with machine. Add eggs one at a time and mix well. Add additional flour 1/2 cup at a time to form a soft dough.

Turn onto a floured surface and knead 8-10 minutes, adding flour as necessary to prevent dough from sticking. Place in a greased bowl and turn to coat. Cover and let rise in a warm place for 30-45 minutes or until volume doubles. Punch down and let rest 5 minutes.

Divide dough into 2 pieces. Roll each piece of dough on a lightly floured surface to a 14- by 12-inch rectangle. Spread half of filling mixture over dough, leaving 1 inch uncovered on a 14-inch side. Roll tightly like a jelly roll and seal edges well. Fold each end 1 1/2 inches under and seal. Repeat with other piece of dough and remaining filling. Place loaves in greased 9- by 5- by 3-inch pans.

Seal opening very well with fingers. Cover and let rise 30-45 minutes in a warm place.

Bake at 375 degrees for 25-30 minutes until lightly browned. Cool.

To make glaze, combine powdered sugar and lemon juice, stirring until smooth. Drizzle lemon glaze over the cooled loaves.

Mexican Swirl Bread
with Jack Cheese and Olives

Yields 2 loaves

Prepare one recipe of the Mexican Enchilada Loaf (p.10), omitting the green chilies. After the first rising, punch down the dough and divide into 2 pieces. Let rest 10 minutes.

Filling:
- 1 cup green pimento-stuffed olives
- 1/2 cup fresh cilantro or parsley leaves
- 1 tablespoon chili powder
- 1 tablespoon olive oil
- 2 cups (8 ounces) shredded Monterey Jack cheese

Combine all ingredients except cheese in a food processor and chop very finely. Add cheese and blend together.

Roll each piece of dough on a lightly floured surface to a 14- by 12-inch rectangle. Spread half of filling mixture over dough, leaving 1 inch uncovered on a 14-inch side. Roll tightly like a jelly roll and seal edges well. Fold each end under 11/2 inches and seal. Repeat with other piece of dough and remaining filling. Place loaves in greased 9- by 5- by 4-inch pans.

Brush tops with olive oil and sprinkle lightly with coarse salt. Bake in a preheated 350-degree oven for 25-35 minutes or until the bread sounds hollow when tapped on the bottom.

Cool before serving.

Lemon Poppy Seed Bread

Yields 1 loaf

3 1/2	cups white bread flour, divided
1/4	cup sugar
2	tablespoons yeast
1	tablespoon salt
	Grated zest of 1 lemon
1/4	cup poppy seeds
1	cup milk
1/4	cup margarine
1	egg
1/2	teaspoon lemon extract

For glaze:

1	tablespoon lemon juice
2	tablespoons sugar

Place 2 cups flour, sugar, yeast, salt, lemon zest, and poppy seeds in a bowl and mix to blend. Heat milk and margarine to 120-130 degrees and add egg and lemon extract. Add wet ingredients to dry ingredients. Mix 2 minutes or 100 strokes by hand. Add additional flour by 1/2 cups until soft dough forms.

Turn out onto a floured surface and knead, adding flour as necessary, until dough is smooth and springs back when pressed with 2 fingers, 8-10 minutes. Place in greased bowl, turn to coat, cover, and let rise for 10 minutes.

Shape into a loaf and place in greased 9- by 5- by 4-inch pan. Cover and let rise 45-60 minutes until dough rises 1 inch over pan.

Bake at 375 degrees for 25-30 minutes until done. Combine lemon juice and sugar. While still warm, spread glaze over bread in pan and let cool.

Unable to bear our catless state, we brought back two kittens from an Indiana farm. Friends down the road remarked, "So, you couldn't find a couple of stray cats in Door County?"

Obviously they had not met THE GIRLS. Like their predecessor, their personalities soon became evident. The double coated grey and white Miss Gilly somehow always seemed to be on everyone's lap at once. Her extreme intelligence led us to speculate on a Ph.D. for her in small mammal zoology, an interest she pursued zealously in the fields around the farm. I think field research took on new meaning. Sensible shoes and an open heart...that was Miss Gilly.

Her sister Willow is another story. Aloof and beautiful in her pure grey coat, she believes she is the great-great-great grand kitten of the Grand Duchess Anastasia's cat; her humble birth being but a slight error. Her plans to become the first inter-species Miss America contestant has her devoting endless hours practicing her runway walk on the overhead beam in the gallery. Bill nailed an apple crate to the wall at the end of the beam so she can sit on a cushion and supervise the day's activities.

One day, six months after getting the girls, Bill walked by the woodshed and heard a suspicious noise in the rafters. Fearing a raccoon or porcupine (or lions and tigers and bears, OH MY), he armed himself with an ax and VERY cautiously climbed the ladder to do battle with whatever critter had set up housekeeping. The ax fell from his hand with the first glance at Mac, a local feral cat and her five newborn kittens. Being no fool of a mom, Mac instantly encouraged the kittens to consider us god-parents. The day they took solid food from us she disappeared without so much as a farewell wave of her tail. She knew the kittens were in good hands.

It became the summer of the kittens. They "helped" us roof the shed, cultivate and fertilize the 48 tomato plants, entertain all visitors, check the homemade ice cream for salt, and picnic with us in the woods. Gilly and Willow took over their feline education teaching them to stalk and hunt. We often found seven cat rears high in the air with tails whipping as critter holes invited close scrutiny. If one of the little kittens so much as flinched they earned a sharp smack with a paw from the older girls.

There were no lack of families waiting to adopt them but one tabby male, Tygge, was determined to become a permanent member of our family. When the back door opened and the girls rushed out, Tygge rushed in. When we took the litter box outside to change it, Tygge would quickly jump in and show us what a fine gentleman he could be if we would just let him in. No one but no one could withstand the assault on our hearts waged by Mr. Tygge. He won.

At eighteen pounds, he is now described as husky, Mr. Chunkers, and a variety of other worthy descriptions. He earns his daily munchies by demonstrating the healthful benefits of relaxation. He spends his days in The Gift to Be Simple Gallery by re-arranging the floral bouquets, entertaining children and impatient husbands, serving as our "second story staff greeter," and enhancing the window displays if there is sun.

Orange Fennel Bread

Yields 1 loaf

31/2	cups white bread flour, divided
1/4	cup sugar
2	tablespoons yeast
1	tablespoon salt
	Grated zest of 2 oranges
1	teaspoon fennel seeds, slightly crushed in a mortar
1	cup milk
1/4	cup margarine
1	egg

For glaze:

1	tablespoon orange juice
2	tablespoons sugar

Place 2 cups flour, sugar, yeast, salt, orange zest, and fennel seeds in a bowl and mix to blend. Heat milk and margarine to 120-130 degrees and add egg. Add wet ingredients to dry ingredients. Mix 2 minutes or 100 strokes by hand. Add additional flour by 1/2 cups until soft dough forms.

Turn out onto a floured surface and knead, adding flour as necessary, until dough is smooth and springs back when pressed with 2 fingers, 8-10 minutes. Place in greased bowl, turn to coat, cover, and let rise for 10 minutes.

Shape into a loaf and place in greased 9- by 5- by 4-inch pan. Cover and let rise 45-60 minutes until dough rises 1 inch over pan.

Bake at 375 degrees for 25-30 minutes until done. Combine orange juice and sugar. While still warm, spread glaze over bread in pan and let cool.

For many years I taught summer dance classes for the University of Wisconsin Extension Peninsula Dance program. Everyone raced from a day at work or arranged schedules to meet at 5:30 to sweat for 90 minutes. Bill accompanied us on the geriatric piano in the historic Fish Creek Town Hall while we gripped the window sills instead of barres and planned our pas de chats around the worst warped, slippery patches on the floor. Compared to the mirrored, properly equipped, smooth-floored studios in which I was accustomed to teaching, the conditions were far from ideal. But somehow, the lake breeze that sailed through the tall old windows, the sight of a red sun being drawn into the bay over the dock and Bill's improvised tunes worked their magic on us. He would provide musical commentary on the progress of the class; a few bars of the "Hallelujah Chorus" always signaled a successful effort and the Ohio State alma mater or Auld Lang Syne to remind me that I was running late. It wasn't exactly a traditional class but it was a very successful and happy one. One student became a principal of the Houston Ballet, three students earned degrees in dance and almost all are still actively studying or performing dance.

Bobbie, the illustrator of this book, was one of these stalwart students and, like the rest, has become a dear friend. Visitors love to watch her paint the flowers and surroundings of our home on bread days. She, like most dancers, loves good bread. Her passion for these bread and chocolate buns was revealed by the game plan she set forth one Thursday as the buns came warm from the oven.

"First, I'll eat this little one just to warm up. Then I'll take a couple of those medium ones and by that time I should be ready for that nice big one over there." Her attention to the buns does not diminish as the afternoon wears on.

So if some Thursday bread day you see a diminutive Peter Pan look-a-like with a paintbrush and chocolate bun, no formal introduction will be necessary.

Bobbie's Chocolate Buns

Yields 32 3-inch buns

5¹/₂-6¹/₂	cups white bread flour, divided
2	tablespoons dry yeast
1	tablespoon salt
¹/₂	cup sugar
2	cups milk
¹/₂	cup margarine
2	eggs
2	teaspoons vanilla extract
1	16-ounce package semi-sweet chocolate chips

For icing:
1	cup powdered sugar
1	tablespoon melted butter or margarine
1	teaspoon vanilla extract
	Milk to thin

Mix 4 cups flour and remaining dry ingredients together. Heat milk and margarine to 140-160 degrees. Margarine does not need to be completely melted. Add milk mixture to dry ingredients and beat 100 stroke or 2 minutes. Add eggs one at a time and mix well. Add vanilla and mix well. Add additional flour ¹/₂ cup at a time to form a soft dough.

Turn onto a floured surface and knead 8-10 minutes, adding flour as necessary to prevent dough from sticking. Place in a greased bowl and turn to coat. Cover and let rise in a warm place for 30-45 minutes or until volume doubles. Punch down and let rest 5 minutes.

Divide dough into 32 pieces. Roll each piece into a ball then stretch dough into 3-inch-diameter circle. Place 7 or 8 chocolate chips in the center of the dough and pull edges up to make a ball. Seal opening very well with fingers.

Place on greased cookie sheets. Cover and let rise 30-45 minutes in a warm place.

Bake at 325 degrees for 12-15 minutes until lightly browned. Cool.

To make glaze, combine powdered sugar, butter and vanilla with a small amount of milk. Stir and add milk until glaze is smooth. Drizzle glaze over cooled buns.

Finnish Biscuit Bread

Yields 4 braided loaves

3 1/2	cups milk
2	ounces fresh or 2 1/4-ounce packages dry yeast
1 1/3	cups plus 1/4 cup sugar, divided
1/2	cup lukewarm water (90-100 degrees)
14-15	cups white flour, divided
1	teaspoon salt
4	eggs, beaten
2/3	cup softened butter
10	cardamom seeds, hulled and crushed

For brushing:
1/2	cup sugar
2	tablespoons water

Scald milk in saucepan, heating until small bubbles appear around edge. Set aside to cool to 110-120 degrees.

Dissolve yeast and 1/4 cup sugar in water. Combine yeast mixture, 4 cups flour, milk and remaining ingredients to make a sponge. Let sponge rise until doubled in volume, about 1/2 hour. Add flour gradually until dough is soft and elastic but not sticky. The last part of the flour will need to be worked in with your hands. A separate kneading is not necessary. Let rise until doubled in volume.

Divide into 4 parts. Make 3 ropes out of each part. Braid into a loaf and seal ends. Let loaves rise 30-40 minutes. Bake 35 minutes in 350-degree oven.

Remove to cooling racks. Combine sugar and water and brush tops of loaves while loaves are still warm.

Coffee Crescent with Variations

Yields 3 crescent rings

1	cup butter or margarine
1	tablespoon sugar
3	egg yolks, beaten
1	1/4-ounce package dry yeast
1	cup lukewarm milk (90-100 degrees)
4	cups flour
1	teaspoon salt
1	12-ounce can Solo brand apricot or almond filling
	Cinnamon
	Chopped nuts

For filling:

3	egg whites
1	cup sugar

For icing:

1 1/2	cups powdered sugar
1	teaspoon vanilla extract
1/4	cup lukewarm evaporated milk (90-100 degrees)

Cream butter, sugar, and eggs until smooth. Dissolve yeast in milk. Add flour and salt alternately with milk and yeast to creamed mixture. Mix by hand until stiff. Refrigerate overnight. Do not be concerned if dough does not rise very much.

The next day, make filling by beating egg whites until stiff but not dry. Slowly add sugar while beating. Set aside.

Divide dough into 3 sections. Roll out each section into a 1/4-inch thick rectangle. Spread 1/3 of apricot or almond filling over section, leaving space at the edges. Fill each section with 1/3 of meringue filling, leaving space at the edges. Sprinkle with cinnamon and chopped nuts.

Roll filled dough like a jelly roll. Place seam side down, curve into a crescent, and place on greased pie plate.

Bake 40 minutes in 325-degree oven or until lightly golden. Let cool slightly.

To make icing, combine sugar, vanilla, and milk; stir until smooth. Drizzle over rings.

Chocolate Chip Christmas Loaf

Yields 1 loaf

13/4	cups sifted all purpose flour
3	teaspoons double acting baking powder
1/2	teaspoon salt
1	teaspoon cinnamon
1/2	teaspoon nutmeg
1	cup (6 ounces) chocolate chips
3/4	cup rolled oats, regular or quick cooking
1	egg
3/4	cup sugar
1	cup milk
1/4	cup corn oil margarine, melted

For frosting:

1	tablespoon butter or margarine
1	cup powdered sugar
1/4	teaspoon vanilla extract
	Milk to thin

Preheat oven to 350 degrees. Grease a 9- by 5- by 4-inch loaf pan.

Mix flour, baking powder, and salt. Add spices, chocolate chips and oats. Beat together egg, sugar, milk, and melted margarine. Add liquid mixture to dry mixture and stir until all ingredients are moistened.

Pour into prepared loaf pan and bake 1 hour or until a toothpick inserted into the middle comes out clean. Turn out of pan at once and let cool.

To make frosting, combine butter, powdered sugar and vanilla, stirring in only enough milk to thin the frosting. Drizzle icing over cooled bread.

This recipe is easily doubled.

Apricot Pockets

Yields 32 3-inch buns

5 1/2-6 1/2	cups white bread flour, divided
2	tablespoons dry yeast
1	teaspoon salt
1/2	cup sugar
	Grated zest of 1 lemon
1/2	cup chopped dried apricots
1/2	cup margarine
2	cups milk or 1 cup milk and 1 cup apricot nectar
2	eggs
1	10-ounce jar apricot spreadable fruit

For glaze:

1	cup powdered sugar
3	tablespoons lemon juice

Mix 4 cups flour, yeast, salt, sugar, zest, and apricots in large bowl. Heat margarine and milk to 140-160 degrees. Margarine does not need to be completely melted. Add milk mixture to dry ingredients and beat 100 strokes or 2 minutes. Add eggs one at a time and mix well. Add additional flour 1/2 cup at a time to form a soft dough.

Turn onto a floured surface and knead 8-10 minutes, adding flour as necessary to prevent the dough from sticking. Place in a greased bowl and turn to coat. Cover and let rise in a warm place for 30-45 minutes or until the volume doubles. Punch down and let rest 5 minutes.

Divide dough into 32 pieces. Roll each piece into a ball then stretch dough into 3-inch-diameter circle. Place 1 measuring tablespoon of jam in the center of the dough and pull edges up to make a ball. Seal opening very well with fingers. Place on greased cookie sheets. Cover and let rise 30-45 minutes in a warm place.

Bake at 325 degrees for 12-15 minutes until lightly browned. Cool.

To make glaze, combine powdered sugar and lemon juice, stirring until smooth. Drizzle lemon glaze over cooled buns.

These brownies are from Gloria Hardiman's recipe file. Although they are officially called Deep Dish Brownies, they have been forever christened "Killer Brownies" by my students at UW-Green Bay who request "those killer brownies of yours" for organizational bake sales and special occasions. They have the youthful metabolism and schedules of dance classes, aerobics, theatre productions, and dance team rehearsals to consume the calories without conscience. On the other hand, Gloria and I combat our raging mutual chocoholism with dutifully observed early morning exercise sessions. We do the steps with Gin Miller, we lift the weights with Jane Fonda, and stretch and contract. Even George and Bill have been affected. They now work out at the health club before splitting breakfast entrees and harassing waitresses at various local cafes.

Gloria's Killer Brownies

3/4	cup melted butter
1 1/2	cups sugar
1 1/2	teaspoons vanilla extract
3	eggs
3/4	cup all purpose flour
1/2	cup cocoa
1/2	teaspoon baking powder
1/2	teaspoon salt
1	cup chocolate chips

Preheat oven to 350 degrees. Blend melted butter, sugar, and vanilla. Add eggs and beat with a spoon. In separate bowl, combine flour, cocoa, baking powder, and salt. Gradually add dry ingredients to egg mixture, beating until well blended. Stir in chips. Spread in greased 8- by 8- by 2-inch square pan and bake 40-45 minutes. Cool.

For a double recipe use a 9- by 13-inch pan.

Cherry Orchard Tarts

Yields 3 dozen tartlets

1	cup butter or margarine
1	tablespoon sugar
3	egg yolks, beaten
1	package dry yeast
1	cup lukewarm milk (90-100 degrees)
4	cups flour
1	teaspoon salt

For cherry tart filling:

1	16-ounce can cherry pie filling
	Pinch of salt
1/2	teaspoon almond extract
	Dash of nutmeg

For icing:

1 1/2	cups powdered sugar
1	teaspoon vanilla extract
1/4	cup lukewarm evaporated milk

Cream butter, sugar, and eggs until smooth. Dissolve yeast in milk. Add flour and salt alternately with wet ingredients to creamed mixture. Mix by hand until stiff. Refrigerate overnight. Do not be concerned if dough does not rise very much.

The next day, make filling by mixing pie filling, salt, almond extract, and nutmeg until blended. Set aside.

Divide dough into 3 sections. Roll out each section into a 1/4-inch thick rectangle. Cut into 2-inch squares (12 pieces). Fill each square with 1 teaspoon cherry filling and pinch diagonal corners tightly together.

Bake 20 minutes in 325-degree oven or until lightly golden. Let cool slightly.

To make icing, combine sugar, vanilla, and milk; stir until smooth. Drizzle over tarts.

Lemon Cream Loaf

Yields 2 loaves

1/2	cup margarine
11/4	cups sugar
2	eggs, unbeaten
21/4	cups flour
3	teaspoons baking powder
1	teaspoon salt
2	tablespoons grated fresh lemon rind
3/4	cup evaporated milk
1/4	cup water
1	8-ounce package cream cheese cut into 1/4-inch cubes
1/2	cup chopped walnuts

For glaze:

1/3	cup sugar
1/4	cup fresh lemon juice

Cream margarine and sugar until smooth. Add eggs and blend together. In separate bowl, combine flour, baking powder, salt and lemon rind. In another bowl, combine evaporated milk and water. Add flour mixture alternately with milk and water to creamed mixture. Fold cream cheese and walnuts in by hand.

Pour into 2 greased 8- by 4-inch bread pans. Bake at 375 degrees for 45-55 minutes.

After baking, combine sugar and fresh lemon juice and brush over tops of loaves.

Leave bread in pans for 30 minutes before removing.

Oatmeal Bread with Applesauce, Cherry, and Peach Variations

Yields 2 loaves

1	cup oatmeal, regular or quick cooking
1	cup whole wheat flour
4-4¹/₂	cups white bread flour, divided
2	tablespoons dry yeast
1	teaspoon salt
1/4	cup sugar plus additional sugar for topping
2	cups cherry applesauce or 2 cups applesauce and 1 3-ounce package cherry gelatin
1/4	cup margarine
1	egg
1	teaspoon almond extract
1/2	cup dried Door County cherries
	Milk for topping

Blend together oatmeal, whole wheat flour, 2 cups bread flour, yeast, salt, and sugar.

Heat together applesauce or applesauce and gelatin mixture and margarine to 120-130 degrees. Margarine does not need to melt. Add to dry ingredients and mix for 2 minutes by machine or hand. Add egg, almond extract, and dried cherries and mix for 1 minute. Add additional flour by 1/2 cups until a soft dough forms.

Turn dough onto floured surface and knead for 10-12 minutes. This is a stiffer, heavier dough so if you get tired, just leave dough for a few minutes and then resume kneading. The dough doesn't care.

Place dough in greased bowl and turn to coat. Cover and let rise 1-11/2 hours in a warm place. Punch down, divide dough and shape into 2 loaves. Place in 2 greased 9- by 4- by 3-inch pans. Let rise until doubled in volume. Brush tops with milk and lightly sprinkle with sugar.

Bake at 350 degrees for 30-35 minutes. Cool before slicing.

Variations:
Use plain applesauce. Replace dried cherries with dried apples and add 1 teaspoon cinnamon and 1 teaspoon vanilla extract.

Use peach applesauce or regular applesauce and 1 package of peach gelatin. Replace dried cherries with dried peaches and add 1 teaspoon cinnamon and 1/2 teaspoon grated lemon rind.

Note: The addition of gelatin adds strong color to the bread. A gentler color will result from using the flavored applesauce.

Swedish Coffee Cake

Yields 3 braided coffee cakes

1	cup evaporated milk
1/2	cup butter plus additional butter, melted, for coating
3	eggs
3/4	cup sugar, divided
1	teaspoon salt
1	package dry yeast
1/4	cup warm water (105-110 degrees)
1	tablespoon cardamom ground
1	lemon rind, grated
41/2	cups white all purpose flour
1	teaspoon cinnamon
1	cup slivered almonds

Heat milk and butter until scalded; small bubbles will appear around edges. Set aside. Beat eggs, 1/2 cup sugar, and salt until well blended. Dissolve yeast in water. Add yeast, water, cardamom, and lemon rind to egg mixture. Add milk and butter. Stir in flour until well mixed. Let rise until doubled in volume.

Punch down and refrigerate for several hours to allow dough to stiffen while it rises.

Divide dough into 3 parts. Roll each part into a rectangle and cut into 3 strips (ropes). Braid the 3 strips and put on a cookie sheet. Brush dough with melted butter. Combine cinnamon and remaining 1/4 cup sugar and sprinkle 1/3 of mixture over butter. Push 1/3 of slivered almonds into cracks of braids. Let rise until doubled in volume. Repeat for remaining 2 pieces of dough.

Bake in preheated 350-degree oven for 20 minutes. Let cool before serving.

Recipe for a Door County Food Fight

This food fight celebration was to "honor" the birthday of Carol's sister, Patti Brandt. The odd Door County rituals surrounding birthdays take many other diverse forms. Our friend Dan was particularly unenthusiastic about having grown a year older and clearly let it be known that he wanted to sit in his backyard with the June mosquitoes, smoke a pipe and drink a beer. To Nancy, Carol and I, this request was not in the best interest of either Dan or the three of us. We flat out disregarded Dan and set up a commando raid on the birthday boy.

It is absolutely astounding that three very middle-aged adults wearing panty hose masks (Nancy's were commandeered) can drive down a state highway, through two towns, without ever having anyone look askance. We coasted into Dan's driveway and crawled on our bellies up to the lawn chair in which he quietly sat smoking and enjoying his privacy. Without so much as a word, we grabbed various body parts and dragged poor old Dan into the car, leaving a trail of change from his pockets on the lawn for Darlene his companion to follow.

Not many of our friends tell us when they are having birthdays anymore.

1	sister celebrating her 40th birthday
2	stressed out goldsmiths*
1	mortified 13-year-old**
2	shop owners with tired faces and feet
1	backyard (large and secluded)
1	dozen raw eggs hidden in apple tree limbs and thither and yon
	Mashed potatoes
	Cooked spaghetti
	Maple syrup
	Rice pudding
	Ketchup
	Mustard
	Whipped cream in cans
	Jell-o in assorted flavors
	Squirt guns
	Prepared vanilla pudding
	Honey in plastic bottles

Assemble all ingredients on a picnic table. Agree on ground rules to be broken (optional).

Eat normal nutritious dinner for strength.

Slyly flip one spoonful of potatoes across the table to start the process. Whip all above ingredients into a frenzy. Decorate all participants liberally as desired. Serve without inhibition but lots of laughter.

Forcefully apply water from garden hose to cool the entire concoction, clean the area and all participants.

Top with coffee, brandy or hot chocolate.

Note: After serving this particular creation in story form to our other friends, they have divided into three distinct groups. Group 1 consists of those who insist on being invited when we do it again. Group 2 consists of those who wouldn't come if we offered cash and Group 3 includes those who want to videotape the sequel!

*Paul and Anne Lings
**Mary, their daughter

Focaccia with
Herb, Tomato and Olive Variations

Yields 2 round flat loaves

2 cups semolina flour	Topping choices:
4 cups white bread flour, divided	Kosher salt
2 tablespoons dry yeast	Pitted olives
1 tablespoon coarse salt	Oil marinated sundried tomatoes
2 tablespoons sugar	Olive tapenade
2 cups water	Fresh herbs, especially
6 tablespoons olive oil	rosemary leaves
Additional olive oil for brushing	Roasted garlic cloves
	Roasted shallot cloves

Mix semolina and 2 cups white bread flour, yeast, salt, and sugar in large bowl. Heat water to 120-130 degrees. Add liquid and olive oil to dry ingredients and mix well, 2 minutes by electric mixer or 100 strong strokes by hand. Add additional flour, 1/2 cup at a time, until soft dough forms.

Turn onto a floured surface and knead 5-7 minutes, adding flour as necessary. Divide into 2 pieces. Let rest 10 minutes. Roll each piece into a 10-inch circle on a floured surface. A baking peel or cookie sheet works best. With a sharp knife or razor blade, slash down 1/4- to 1/2-inch at 1-inch intervals. Turn dough halfway around and repeat the slashing to form a checkerboard pattern. Cover loaves and let rise 30 minutes. Brush loaves with additional olive oil. Add toppings.

For a simple bread, sprinkle with salt, pitted olives, and rosemary leaves. For other variations try oil marinated sundried tomatoes, olive Tapenade (p. 50), or put one topping on one side and a different topping on the other. Wait until the last 5 minutes or so of the baking to spread tomatoes or tapenade as they have a tendency to burn at baking temperatures.

Another variation, a combination of roasted garlic and shallot cloves, pitted Greek olives, and fresh sprigs of herbs, is also delicious.

Bake at 400 degrees on baking tiles for 10-15 minutes.

Serve with saucers of olive oil and dip bread into oil. Make sure to use the highest quality olive oil. This is not the place for an inexpensive oil.

Open Flame Pizza with Variations

We have two campsites that we hide on The Gift to Be Simple land. One is deep in the middle of the pine tree forest behind the house, and the other is across the road sheltered in a crescent of trees overlooking a meadow. At both sites, we have a plain tripod with an attached grill hanging over a firepit made from stones from the fence row. Many summer meals are cooked over an open flame by the glow of the full moon. We have developed ways to cook on the grill over open flame that result in delicately smoky refined pizza. One can use a Weber-type grill with the same flavor results but the ambiance is worth an open fire.

Herbed Pizza Crust

Yields 2 crusts

$1/2$	cup organic whole wheat bread flour
$11/2$	cups semolina flour
4	cups white bread flour, divided
2	tablespoons dry yeast
2	teaspoons dried rosemary, finely crushed
1	teaspoon dried garlic powder
2	cups water
2	tablespoons olive oil
	Additional flour for dusting

Combine whole wheat flour, semolina, 2 cups white bread flour, yeast, rosemary, and garlic powder in large bowl. Heat water to 120-130 degrees. Add water and olive oil to dry ingredients and mix well, 2 minutes by electric mixer or 100 strong strokes by hand. Add additional bread flour by $1/2$ cups as necessary until soft dough forms.

Turn dough onto a floured surface and knead 10-12 minutes or until dough springs back when pressed with 2 fingers, adding flour as necessary. Put dough into oiled bowl, turn to coat surface, and cover with damp towel or plastic wrap. Let rise in warm place until doubled in volume. Punch down, knead briefly, 10-15 strokes, and let it rest.

If you are making the pizza in an oven instead of on an open fire, preheat oven to 450 degrees and place baking stones or tiles in oven 45-60 minutes before baking. Divide dough in half and let rest 10 minutes. Roll each piece into a 10-inch circle on a floured surface. A bakers peel or cookie sheet works best.

Top with toppings and bake for 10-15 minutes

Semolina Pizza Dough

Yields 2 crusts

2	cups semolina flour
4	cups white bread flour, divided
2	tablespoons yeast
2	tablespoons sugar
1	tablespoon coarse salt
2	cups water
6	tablespoons olive oil

Combine semolina and 2 cups white bread flour, yeast, sugar, salt and sugar in large bowl. Heat water to 120-130 degrees. Add water and olive oil to the dry ingredients and mix well, 2 minutes by electric mixer or 100 strong strokes by hand. Add additional bread flour by 1/2 cups as necessary until soft dough forms.

Turn dough onto a floured surface and knead 10-12 minutes or until dough springs back when pressed with 2 fingers, adding flour as necessary. Put dough into oiled bowl, turn to coat surface, and cover with damp towel or plastic wrap. Let rise in warm place until doubled in volume. Punch down, knead briefly, 10-15 strokes, and let it rest.

Continue following directions for Herbed Pizza Dough.

To Cook Over Open Flame or on a Grill

Have dough rolled out on heavy duty aluminum foil. The grill should be approximately 1 foot above the open flame. If a Weber-type grill is used, place the grill in its highest position. Quickly invert dough directly onto the grill. A pair of barbecue tongs is of great aid. Let cook until bottom is firm, about 5-10 minutes.

Invert the crust over the fire and cook until the other side is firm. Remove from fire and cover with the toppings of your choice. Slide back onto the grill and cover with foil or a wok pan lid.

Bake until cheese is melted.

Toppings

We have found that limiting the number and quantity of ingredients allows the flavor of each ingredient to develop fully. Do not overload the pizza.

Brie cheese with fresh spinach leaves, red onion rings and pecans

Jack cheese with peppers, drained can corn, black beans, salsa, stuffed green olives and cilantro

Smoked cheddar cheese with ham or bacon, and fresh spinach

Feta cheese with Greek olives, artichoke hearts, garlic and anchovy (optional)

Brie with smoked salmon, caramelized onions and dill

Provolone and gorgonzola cheeses with sundried tomatoes in oil, roasted and fresh tomatoes and fresh basil leaves

Parmesan cheese, roasted potato, grilled zucchini, grilled onion and fresh rosemary

Fontina and shaved Parmesan cheeses with pesto, red onion, fresh spinach and slivered almonds

Fontina, gorgonzola, bel paese and Parmesan cheeses

Noise

In our neighborhood we go without many things. We don't have any fast-food restaurants or sidewalks or fences or neon and the loudest noise is the dump truck changing gears as it goes around the corner. A siren breaks the sound of birds and tree frogs maybe twice a summer. And yet we, like city folks, do have a great problem with noise. Down the road is a small grass airport used by a small private plane and two ultralights. The ultralights have motors that sound like Lawnboy mowers after just coming out of high grass. The giant gnat buzzes and whines over our heads while we work in the gardens or sit under the trees at our campsite. But the greatest noise problem comes when the pilot cuts the engine to show the airworthiness of the canvas and conduit craft. Why should I care if he goes away and yet every time...every single time the mosquito stops buzzing, I snap my head skyward willing the bug to be alive. After a short growl, I take myself in hand and realize the absurdity of my complaint. One ultralight...maybe when I look up I should just say thanks for reminding me of what we don't have.

Things to Make Bread Less Alone

At the end of the day, George and Gloria bike down from their Maple Grove Gallery, or Lynn drops by after a charter on The Fish Doctor. If not, Cousin Bruce ambles by or Pastor Dan or Bobbie and Richard or Cindy or...or...Our summer nights are filled with dear friends with whom we share stories of the days' events. After Thursday bread day demonstrations, they know we always keep several special loaves of bread in reserve for just this time. A simple dip, an olive or veggie appetizer or two, a glass of wine and the celebration is on.

The recipes that follow go well with breads. In some cases, the bread loaves can be cut into 1/4 inch rounds and dried for 30 minutes or so in a 250-degree oven to make cocktail melbas. Like the Middle eastern mezze or the Spanish tapas, a little of many things makes a powerful stimulant to conversation and friendship.

Aunt Zola's Curried Olives

3	tablespoons lemon juice
3	tablespoons curry powder
3/4	cup salad oil
1	cup finely chopped green onion
2	cups drained, stuffed olives

Combine lemon juice and curry powder in food processor. Gradually add oil until blended.

Add onions and pour over olives. Let stand overnight in covered bowl or jar in refrigerator to develop full flavor. Any leftover marinade is fantastic on a salad.

My Aunt Zola was like an Auntie Mame. She could turn a 5 p.m. visit into an ad hoc hors d'oeuvre party with the flash of a freezer door. These olives are so addictive that my cousin Bruce said he would eat rubber erasers if they were in the curry marinade. There is nothing "hot" in this curry.

Roasted Sweet Red Pepper Butter

Yields 1 1/2 cups

1/2	of a 15-ounce jar roasted red peppers
1/2	large red onion
2	cloves garlic
1	jalapeno pepper
1	green chili, canned
	Juice of 1/2 lemon
1	tablespoon Tabasco sauce
2	tablespoons chili powder
1	cup butter or margarine

The combination of peppers produces great depth of flavor without exceptional heat. Captain Lynn Frederick has been known to stop by at the end of bread day with a fresh salmon off her boat. A meal of charcoal grilled salmon, over a bed of fettuccine, topped with red pepper butter, fresh greens salad, bread and a summer sunset is pure bliss.

Combine all ingredients except butter in food processor for 1 1/2 minutes. Add butter and process until smooth. The amount of Tabasco and jalapeno can be adjusted to taste.

Serve with thin slices of baguette and a very dry white wine.

Hummus bi Tahini

Yields 2 cups

1	15-ounce can Garbanzo beans (generally available in the Mexican section of the market)
2-3	cloves garlic, peeled
1/2	cup tahini (ground sesame seed butter)
	Juice of 2-3 lemons
	Salt to taste
	Olive oil for garnish
	Paprika for garnish

Put beans, garlic, tahini, and juice of 2 lemons in food processor. Puree until smooth and creamy. Add salt to taste. If flavor seems too raw or "beany" add more lemon juice until all flavors marry. If mixture becomes too thick, add olive oil until a smooth consistency is reached.

Pour onto a dinner plate. Lightly drizzle good olive oil over top. Sprinkle with paprika.

This is a dip that goes well with any focaccia, herb, or French bread and a glass of hearty red wine.

Black Bean Dip

Yields approximately 3 cups

1	10³/₄ can black bean soup (Campbell's)
2	green onions, coarsely chopped
2	tablespoons chopped fresh cilantro or 2 teaspoons dried
1	teaspoon salt

Add, adjusting to suit your spice and heat tastes:

1	tablespoon Tabasco sauce
2	tablespoons chili garlic sauce
	(available in the oriental section of most markets)

Or substitute:

2	cloves fresh garlic, minced
1-2	fresh jalapeno peppers, seeded and deveined

1	15-ounce can black beans, rinsed and drained
1	8-ounce package cream cheese (no-fat kind works well here)

Put all ingredients except black beans and cream cheese in processor and pulse until pureed. Add black beans and cream cheese and pulse only until well blended. Do not over-process.

If you decide not to add the Tabasco, chili paste or peppers, make sure to add the fresh garlic.

Serve with tortilla chips or Mexican Swirl Bread and cold beer, preferably Negro Modelo or Corona.

Olives in Citrus and Spice Marinade

Yields 4 cups

4 cups assorted olives (any mixture of imported Sicilian greens, Greek olives, Kalamatas, or domestic olives stuffed with garlic, jalapeno, or onion), drained

1/4 cup olive oil

Zest of 1 lemon, finely chopped

Rind of 1/2 orange, finely chopped

Juice of 1 lemon

Juice of 1 orange

2 tablespoons fennel seeds, slightly crushed

1 teaspoon dried red pepper flakes

Put all ingredients in covered bowl. Shake to mix. Refrigerate overnight to blend flavors.

Invert occasionally.

Bring to room temperature to serve.

Feta Cheese Spread

Yields approximately 2 cups

1 teaspoon coarsely ground black pepper

1 8-ounce package cream cheese

1 8-ounce package Athena brand Feta Cheese with Basil and Tomato or substitute:

    8 ounces feta cheese

    1 teaspoon dried basil

    1 teaspoon finely chopped sundried tomato

Blend all ingredients by hand or in a food processor until buttery.

Serve with dried bread chips, Kalamata, Sicilian, or Moroccan olives, and a robust red wine.

Taramasalata

Yields approximately 2 cups

Before you get too far and read tarama, may I explain that this is an inexpensive caviar-type product from carp. The jars of reddish gold can be found in specialty stores, Middle Eastern markets and even Asian markets. The Scandinavians have a carp roe paste in a squeeze tube which works as well. The end result is a very delicate caviar-flavored mayonnaise. This is wonderful as a dip for Sundried Tomato Olive Loaves or Focaccia with Herbs.

1	small onion
1/3	of 8-ounce jar tarama (carp roe)
1-2	cups olive oil
4-5	slices white bread with crusts trimmed
1	cup milk
	Juice of 2-3 lemons

Put onion, tarama, and a little olive oil into processor and blend until smooth. Soak bread in milk and squeeze out excess. With processor running, alternately add bread, remaining olive oil, and lemon juice to tarama mixture until a creamy mayonnaise develops. Adjust taste with lemon juice.

Locks

Life in this place is full of contradictions. One of the more telling contradictions happened to Bill, the potter who demonstrates on bread day. Bill's wife went home one day and found the house locked. Now to folks in the city, this is as it should be. People in the city dare not get out of the habit of locking up all their possessions. They even pull out their beeper equipped car keys and engage the alarm system when they pull in the driveway of our gallery. What a sadness!

But back to Bill and his wife. Neither one of them even knew where their house keys were or if in fact they had any. And now the house was locked front and back. After receiving a breathless call, three police cars came screeching to a halt in front of the house. All the officers agreed with Bill and his wife that it was mighty suspicious for the house to be locked. Why would any one do such a thing and upset the UPS man who put packages in the kitchen or the friend who came to borrow a tool while you are out. They worked their way into the house and searched it from top to bottom to no avail. Bill and his wife spent a cautious night wondering how their house could get locked.

Life is grand when insecurity is finding your house safely locked.

Flavored Butters

Yields 1/2 cup

Butter, especially unsalted butter, is a marvelous carrier of flavor. In this day of low fat everything, one pat of rich butter can be like a whole cheesecake to one who is fat deprived. If you must continue to watch fat intake, soft margarine will work but never as well. On bread days, we have two or three different herbed butters setting next to the nine different breads we bake. The flavoring of butters is very simple. You just have to remember to do it.

To 1/2 cup butter, add any of the following:

2 tablespoons chopped fresh herbs such as:
Thyme (stems removed)
Basil leaves (the little globe basil works well)
Chives (use the lavender thistle head
  as garnish)
Summer savory
Tarragon leaves
Cilantro (also called coriander)
Rosemary leaves
Marjoram leaves

Sometimes stronger flavors are good accents for plainer breads. Be careful not to have the butter compete with the flavors of the bread.

To 1/2 cup butter, blend any *one* of the following combinations:

2 teaspoons chili powder and 1/2 teaspoon cumin
1 clove of garlic very finely minced, or for a milder taste,
  2 cloves of roasted garlic mashed
3 tablespoons honey and 1 teaspoon cinnamon
4 tablespoons honey and 2 tablespoons jam
  (apricot, peach, cherry)

Tapenade with Variations

Yields 1 cup

    1   cup Moroccan oil cured olives, pitted
  1/4   cup capers
    3   cloves garlic, peeled and smashed
    3   tablespoons chopped fresh parsley, flat Italian preferred
    1   teaspoon chopped fresh rosemary
    1   anchovy, rinsed
    2   tablespoons olive oil

or

    1   cup brined Greek olives, pitted
  1/4   cup capers
    3   cloves garlic
    3   tablespoons chopped fresh parsley
    1   anchovy, rinsed
    2   tablespoons olive oil

or

    1   cup Greek or Sicilian green olives, pitted
  1/4   cup capers
    2   cloves of garlic
  1/4   teaspoon Greek oregano
  1/4   teaspoon rosemary
  1/4   teaspoon thyme
    2   tablespoons olive oil

Zest of 1/2 lemon, finely chopped for garnish
Sprig of rosemary for garnish

For each variation, place all ingredients in food processor. Process until a smooth paste is formed. If the paste is too thick, add olive oil until light in texture.

If you absolutely can't stand the anchovy, omit the poor lad.

Over the two black olive variations, add lemon zest and some of the chopped fresh herb as garnish.

Make sure you use a good variety of olives...heavy on the imported kinds.

Roasted Garlic, Tomato and Veggie Toppings

1	bulb fresh garlic
	Olive oil
	Fresh Roma tomatoes
1	red onion
1	bulb fresh fennel
1	medium eggplant skinned
	Regular salt
	Fresh rosemary sprigs
	Kosher salt

Remove all loose skin from garlic. Brush generously with olive oil. Place on foil-covered baking sheet generously brushed with olive oil.

Cut tomatoes crosswise in half. Remove seeds. Place cut side down on baking sheet.

Peel red onion. Slice into 1/2-inch rounds. Lightly brush with oil and place on baking sheet.

Trim stalk away from fennel bulb. Slice bulb into 1/4-inch rounds and place on baking sheet.

Slice eggplant into 1/2-inch slices. Salt each side and drain on paper towels to remove water from eggplant. Place drained slices on baking sheet.

Scatter fresh rosemary sprigs over vegetables.

Roast all vegetables in 375-degree oven for 30-45 minutes until all are tender and garlic is soft.

Separate onion into rings. Cube eggplant. Break garlic bulb into individual cloves. Arrange vegetables on a large platter with garlic cloves in a small ramekin.

To serve, guests squeeze the roasted garlic onto bread and spread it like butter. Do the same with roasted tomatoes. Top bread with a selection of fennel, onion rings and eggplant. Sprinkle with a pinch of Kosher salt and a leaf or two of rosemary.

...Too Wonderful Beverages to go with the loaf and thou...

Most of the time our family and friends enjoy wine as the beverage of choice. However, some occasions prompt special diversions like the four given here. They are marvelously refreshing additions to campfires, picnics by the shore, or to the congregation of Adirondack chairs under the apple trees in the back yard. As George Hardiman says before meals, "In vino veritas."

White Sangria alias The Punch from Hell

10 servings

1 lemon, thinly sliced
1 orange, thinly sliced
1 lime, thinly sliced
4 ounces triple sec or cointreau
1 apple, sliced
4 fresh strawberries
   Crushed ice
1 750 ml. bottle champagne
   (expense does not improve the result)
1 750 ml. bottle dry white wine

Combine citrus fruit and triple sec in a large pitcher and gently mash together. Add apple and strawberries. Add crushed ice to 3/4 full. Add equal parts of wine and champagne.

Refill wine and champagne as needed.

Stone Fence Sour

Yields 1

   Crushed ice
   Fresh apple cider
2 shots of bourbon
1 slice red apple to garnish
   Soda water

In a 12-ounce tumbler, add ice to fill halfway. Add cider to fill half the glass. Add bourbon and apple and top with soda water. Stir to fizz.

This beverage is pure Door County. The land is defined by stones of all sizes; they are the farmers' best crop. With so many available, it is little wonder that the fences of Door County have such character and history. As for apples, there can be none sweeter than those picked surreptitiously by reaching over the fence to the tree beside the road. Fall air is heady with cider smells and apple scents. It is a fine time to enjoy this beverage.

Peg's Margaritas

Yields 2 GENEROUS cocktails

5 parts golden tequila (Cuervo 1800 is the best)
2 parts triple sec
2 parts cointreau
   Juice of 2 lemons
   Salt
   Ice
1 lime cut into wedges

Combine tequila, triple sec, cointreau and lemon juice in a large pitcher.

If you have time, chill in freezer until ready to serve.

To serve, moisten rim of glasses. Dip rims of glasses into a saucer of salt, although salt is certainly not necessary. Fill glasses with coarsely crushed ice. Pour liquid over ice.

Garnish with a wedge of lime.

Caution: These are not the usual tequila slurpies. These are without a doubt the best margaritas ever...however, they are deceptive. Limit yourself and others to 1 serving each and you will continue to enjoy a full evening of pleasurable activity.

Door County Mai Tai
alias Rhubarb Juice Cocktail

8   cups coarsely chopped rhubarb
5   cups water
2-3 cups sugar depending upon taste

In large saucepan over low heat, simmer rhubarb in water and sugar until completely tender. Stir often to break up fibers. Let cool.

Strain fruit and juice through a fine sieve until only course fibers are left. (If you wish a perfectly clear liquid, line sieve with a dampened cheesecloth or jelly bag.)

Juice may be served alone over ice with or without lemon-lime soda. Juice may also be frozen into a slush and scooped into glasses.

To make the Mai Tai adult version, add 1 shot of dark rum to each 4 ounces of juice.

This is an absolutely spectacularly refreshing summer drink. When Mom and Dad visit us from Indianapolis, Dad loves to conclude a full day of hunting our woods for morel mushrooms with a glass of Door County Mai Tai. Boy, am I glad fathers and sons should do things together.

Carol Hoehn is owner of The Gift To Be Simple Gallery in Fish Creek, Wisconsin. She holds a B.A in Dance from Butler University, professional certification from the Royal Academy of Dance, London and the Imperial Society of Teachers of Dance, and has taught dance at professional schools and universities for over thirty years. In addition, Carol has had a career as a professional dancer and actress. Out of her love for designing costumes have come many of the exotic designs and patterns of clothing she creates for the gallery. Her works have been exhibited in art galleries and private collections nationwide. She is noted for intricate fine textile painting incorporating many of the floral elements native to her Door County home. Baking a variety of wonderful breads and desserts is yet another aspect of her creativity.

Bill Hoehn is co-owner of The Gift To Be Simple Gallery in Fish Creek, Wisconsin. He holds a B.M. in Music Education from Butler University and a M.A. and Ph.D. in Musicology from Ohio State University. He currently teaches music in Sturgeon Bay Public Schools and supports his wife in the gallery business as bookkeeper, grounds keeper, salesman, and cheerleader. He is an excellent cook and a willing test subject for Carol's breads.

Roberta L. Larson, illustrator, resides in Sister Bay, Wisconsin and Oak Park, Illinois. Her watercolors and colored pencil drawings are in private collections in the United States, Canada, the Caribbean and Europe and have been featured on the covers of airline first class menus. She has been exhibiting at The Gift To Be Simple gallery since its inception and enjoys painting in the gardens as shopgoers sample Carol and Bill's bread. Larson has a M.A. in Sociology and national recognition as an authority in racial integration. She is married to a mathematics professor and has one adult son and two step-cats.